MW01006553

# THE AUTHOR'S GUIDE TO COVER DESIGN

STUART BACHE

BOOKS COVERED

# CONTENTS

*To my beautiful wife, Natasha, for all of her support.*

# INTRODUCTION

Whether you are a bestselling romance author or just finishing the first in a series of crime novels, your book cover is the very first impression a reader will have of your book. Why not make it the best first impression possible?

If you are commissioning a book cover designer or even designing the cover yourself, *The Author's Guide to Cover Design* gives you the guidance you need to not only understand the process, but build a strong foundation. I teach you how to write the perfect brief, understand the styles of design that work best for your genre using familiarity theory, use the right typography and find the best images for your cover.

With well over a decade of experience in both traditional and independent publishing, I started my career as a Junior Designer for Hodder & Stoughton, worked as Senior Designer for Puffin Books and HarperCollins, and was Art Director of Oneworld Publications. I have worked across every major genre for a whole host of publishers and authors, including Mark Dawson, Stephen King, John le Carré, S. K.

Tremayne and the Tolkien Estate. I am now the Art Director and founder of Books Covered, where I continue to create market-leading book covers for authors, agents and publishers.

I guide you through the world of cover design, sharing ways of making your cover look professional, teach you the design theories behind concept creation, and giving you loads of tips, tricks and advice from my many years as a book cover designer. And, once you've understood the theory, learn to master the art of cover design with practical tutorials in my course. You can learn more about the course here: selfpublishingformula.com/design

This book is not only a guide to cover design, but it is also an essential tool in your journey to becoming a successful author.

## FOREWORD BY MARK DAWSON

I can't remember when I met Stuart for the first time. I was searching around for a new designer to work on my Milton books, and I think that I saw some of his work in an article in a newspaper. I liked it and, because I can be a pushy bugger when I see something that I want, I emailed and asked whether he was interested in taking on another client. Thankfully for me he said yes, and, since then, we've worked together on over 25 books, together with art for my website, ad campaigns and the logo for my publishing company.

I don't think that it is a coincidence that my books have sold many, many more copies since they've been lucky enough to wear Bache covers. I've sold somewhere between one and two million books at the time of writing, and I attribute a lot of that success in having covers that match the genre that I write in whilst also being beautiful to look at.

One of the lessons that I have learned over the years is that independent authors need their products to be indistinguishable from the products of traditional houses, and, together with editing and formatting, the cover makes up for that most important of trifectas. It's probably the most important of the three because, without an eye-catching cover (or a thumb-stopping ad), you don't get to show off your work.

Stu is knowledgeable and wise, and I quickly learned that my best policy was to give him the brief that he asked for and then get the hell out of the way. We've since worked together on a very well-regarded course for authors who want to do their own covers, and I've enjoyed watching him impart his experience patiently, often going out of the way to be helpful.

This book will be the sort of text that will be referred to again and again as authors progress through their publishing journeys. I'm sure it'll lead to even more authors asking for Stu to work on their covers, but - just to check - writing this foreword means I still get first dibs - right, Stu? Right?

Enjoy the book. Learn loads.

Mark Dawson,
   Salisbury, May 2018

# I

# THE RECIPE FOR A GREAT BOOK COVER

# FAMILIARITY THEORY

Arguably, all commercial design – in its multitude of directions and ideas – comes down to two fundamental principles: fit in or stand out. The urge of almost every client is for their product to stand out against the rest, usually because they equate 'visibility' with 'more sales'... and they are almost always completely wrong.

At the very beginning of every project I always ask for comparative and competitive book cover visuals, usually followed by a promise that I'm not intending to rip somebody else's design off.

These visuals help me accomplish two things:

1. As a designer, I will have a better idea of the aesthetic my client wants (we respond better to visual cues).
2. I can use this aesthetic to see what works well in the genre so that I can emulate it.

And no, emulation isn't just a clever word for 'copy'. A designer can break a design up into its constituent parts and figure out what makes it work. For example, a designer can examine the style of typography, how an image is used to express narrative, whether the covers are illustrated, photographic etc., which colour palettes are predominant in the genre and so on. We can then use these rules to create unique concepts which are also familiar aesthetically to titles within its genre.

Over the years, using this method lead me to coin the phrase 'familiarity theory'.

It is by no means a new theory, but it is an important part of my design process and one that I have been using since the start of my career. It is especially useful if you're a new author who is about to publish their first book.

Allow me to elaborate a little.

I mention in the chapter *That All Important Brief* that both Amazon and major bookstores use techniques and algorithms to try and influence your buying decisions. By placing popular books alongside similar-looking novels, the idea being 'if you like this one then maybe you'll try this one', booksellers utilise familiarity theory at its best. Put simply, we find comfort in positive association and it can help us to make a decision when buying.

We have been sold to using this very technique for a long time; from detergent with their love of blue, white and red packaging to the staggering number of social media platforms using blue thanks to the popularity of Facebook. Possibly one of the best examples are movie posters. There are websites dedicated to the sheer number of similar looking designs: the action thriller with a man running, the romantic comedy with a couple lying in bed, or the entire cast of a superhero or sci-fi movie piled on one another in an illustrated style (and you can thank *Star Wars* for that one). Sure, we can laugh, but the reason movie execs with their millions use these tropes is because they are super-effective. In a split second you know the tone, genre and sometimes the entire cast of the movie.

You may be thinking *'But not everything can look alike. Won't my book just blend into the background?'* To answer that, let's look at another example.

Action thrillers such as Mark Dawson and Lee Child's novels share similar tropes and layouts. Their names are large, the font is a condensed sans serif, and they show narrative by putting their protagonist in a scene or setting from the story. Yet, put them side by side, and they have their own presence and identity.

Emulation is not copying. It is using what works in it's market (typography, image style etc.) in a new way.

## WHEN FAMILIARITY THEORY DOESN'T WORK

The evil twin of familiarity theory is 'the big rip-off' which, if you're not careful, is what your cover could end up being.

I've worked with many clients, from self-published authors to editors and marketing departments for big publishers, who want direct copies of the cover from a bestselling book. I used to think they meant 'emulate' but soon realised they literally meant 'take this cover and just change the name and title'. I've even had people add my portfolio site to their 99Designs brief with a 'copy this' link attached to it.

This is both a misunderstanding of how the design process works and complete and utter laziness. When we do this, we are not understanding what makes a particular book sell well, and we are not informing ourselves what works in a market or why a reader buys one book over another; we are just clinging onto a bandwagon and hoping it will take us with it.

# THAT ALL IMPORTANT BRIEF

It's a good idea to put a brief together as soon as you can. A brief will help you focus on what works within your genre and how best to market your book. Completing your brief early on in the process can also aid you in choosing the best designer based on their previous work and style. However, even if you're designing the cover yourself, already having a brief will still be beneficial as you will have everything ready before you begin the design process.

Always bear in mind that a brief is for reference, direction, and ideas only. It is a starting point for your designer and a focal point for you – it is never a rigid set of rules. Narrative is important, especially so in commercial fiction, but knowing the exact dimensions and shape of your heroine's dimple or how her fringe falls across her forehead isn't. Please try to be flexible with your designer and allow them to be creative. You will get a much better cover as a result.

## LET'S GO SHOPPING

Before we start laying out your brief, we need to know a bit more about your genre, and this couldn't be simpler.

Your first port of call should be both Amazon – other online book retailers are available – and your local book shop (it's good to stretch the legs every once in a while) and head to the bestsellers in your genre. Here you will find what's working, what styles are popular, what you're fighting against and, just as importantly, fitting in with. You could make a Pinterest page of your research, click and drag the covers to a folder on your desktop, or scribble a few notes in a pad.

Obviously, there are many more books in the world than those sitting on the bestseller lists and shelves. You could even say that there are arguably better books that are not in those places. As a book cover designer and a business owner, I know what it feels like to want your work be unique, to standout and to work on its own merits. However, I also know the difficulties in selling a product in a saturated market and having to jostle amongst books with bigger budgets and marketing spend. Emulating a bestselling book, especially at the beginning of your career as an author, is not only sensible but saves you a lot of time and money (see the chapter on *Familiarity Theory* for more details). When you're super famous and only need to add your name to your book for it to sell a million copies, then you can do whatever you like!

**Pro-tip:**

1. Whilst you're on Amazon, select some of those bestsellers and browse the 'Sponsored products

related to this item', 'Frequently bought together', and the 'Customers who bought this also bought' sections. These are built on algorithms to make you buy similar products. They're basically free information on how to sell your book.

2. Many large bookshops have a similar approach (in fact, they invented it). Booksellers have spent a lot of time thinking about how to sell you as many books as possible. Waterstones here in the UK will often set up tables with a few bestsellers/well-known titles and surround them with books that have the same themes and aesthetics. In other words, they are trying to make you see a link between those books and its popular sibling and hoping you will buy it.

## WHAT'S IT ALL ABOUT?

Now you have an idea of what works in your market from a visual perspective, we need to disseminate this information into something that will work effectively in brief format (this is especially important if you're creating your own book cover).

Grab a pen and some paper then answer these questions:

- What kind of typography do they use for the title and author name? For example, action thrillers and crime have a proclivity for condensed fonts, such as DIN Condensed, as you can make it larger and create more impact – you can learn more in the chapter *Typefaces: the Good and the (Very) Bad*.

- What style of imagery is it? Is it illustrated, photographic, type-led or perhaps a mix of all of them?
- What are the common themes? They could show an image of running women or men in a location from the story, a much more visceral image with splats of blood or a simple illustration of silhouettes and hearts with bright colours.

These notes will give you a basic outline of what your book cover should convey. Here are some examples:

**Crime thriller**

- Condensed typography.
- Photographic imagery often with texture added.
- Abstract close-up images such as murder scenes, weapons, blood or broken glass.

**Historical romance**

- Serifs or calligraphy.
- Photographic, occasionally sepia or monotone.
- Woman dressed in period costume, either in the scene or the scene is superimposed over them.

**Self-help**

- Sans serif.

- Usually type-led on a clean background (one colour).
- Often an illustration or photograph relating to the topic.

You've done your research, so now you have an idea what your book cover should say and what works within your genre. Lets write this brief. The first few lines are super simple:

- **Title**
- **Subtitle** (if you have one)
- **Author name**
- **Short synopsis**

If you're unsure how detailed your synopsis should be, I often recommend using your back cover blurb (or something similar if you are yet to write it) as it explains the story and lead characters in a snappy way without going into too much detail.

Next up you need to go into a few specifics.

- **Fiction**: Details of important characters (a general idea of what they look like), places and scenes.
- **Non-fiction**: What is the key point of your book? If you're writing a cook book, what style of food is it? If it's self-help, what's the topic?

Finally, add those comparative and competitive book covers you researched earlier. Specifically, those that you would be happy to see bear your own title and name. Designers are visual creatures, so we will better understand the aesthetic you want to achieve from an image far easier than a description.

With the final added touch of book cover examples, your designer should have everything they need to know and you will both be reading from the same page. However, if you have yet to choose a designer, your new brief is a great way to help you find the right one as it can also work as a style-guide to filter through portfolios.

# QUALITY, QUALITY, QUALITY

Invest in quality at the very beginning of your project to get the most from your book cover. Choose a professional designer. If you're designing the cover yourself, buy images of a decent standard, use professional, well-designed typefaces over the standard selection on your PC and work with a proper design application. We will discuss these aspects of designing your own cover in the *How to Design a Book Cover* chapter.

This may seem an obvious and simple point to make, but it is amazing how often it is neglected. Usually, it's because budgets are very tight. You have so many other services to think about (such as editorial and marketing) but it is a misconception that quality must also mean expensive, and a good cover is worth its weight in gold.

*'But those are just words, Stu. I still can't afford a super-awesome cover on my budget.'*

I understand. I too was on a limited budget when I first became a freelance designer. I needed to buy font collections, find the money for image library subscriptions, buy

Photoshop… the list went on. However, it was during those first few fallow months that I learned this important lesson: invest in one, budget on the rest.

This way, you are building a foundation to grow from with the potential of adding quality at each stage, rather than compromising on everything.

With that in mind, let's run through each point and discuss your choices:

## CHOOSE A PROFESSIONAL DESIGNER

By choosing a professional designer you are investing in more than just a good-looking cover, because they will find the right images and typography. They will also have experience in applications such as Photoshop. Ticks all the boxes, right?

Just make sure you choose the right one. Other than a long-term subscription to Adobe, this is the biggest investment you will make, so you need to be sure. A designer with book cover experience is different than one who works in branding (and is a million miles away from your nephew who's 'pretty good at Microsoft Paint').

If you want to use a designer but still find the costs of a professional too high, there are alternatives: you could use a resource such as 99Designs, buy a pre-made cover (where they change the name and title to match yours), or design it yourself.

Don't worry. I go into much more detail about how to choose the right person for the job in *Designers and Where to Find Them*.

## BUY DECENT IMAGES

You can buy fantastic, unique photographs from sources such as Getty, Arcangel Images, and Trevillion. Exclusive usage rights span from five years upwards (after which you will either have to relicense for exclusivity or allow other books to use the image). You can choose which countries or territories you're selling in and how many copies you think you will produce (the minimum tends to be 5000). All of this information will determine how much it will cost you. A single rights-managed photograph with worldwide usage for five years can cost £250/$330 minimum, which may sound expensive but only you can use the image across the entire planet for a whole five years.

If that is too much of a hit, there are sites that also offer royalty-free images at a lower cost.

The more affordable and non-exclusive options are sources like Shutterstock and iStock. They offer either monthly/annual subscriptions, or you can purchase images in sets of five and twenty-five. I have been using Shutterstock as an affordable equivalent for many years, and I can honestly say that it continues to improve. Gone are the days of searching through literally hundreds of images for something half-decent, which is due to the host of talented creatives adding their work to the site on a continual basis.

Whatever you decide, never use clipart found on your PC or photographs you've found on Google.

I explain the difference between rights-managed and royalty-free images, as well as where you can find images, in the chapter on *Picture Research*.

## USE PROFESSIONAL TYPEFACES

A quick browse of MyFonts.com will both amaze and scare you. You will be amazed at how many wonderful typefaces there are, and scared at the cost. However, there are font staples that all designers keep in their arsenal. Typefaces such as Helvetica, Trade Gothic, and Futura are put to good use time and again for crime and thriller. Adobe Garamond, Bodoni, and Didot are often adorning the covers of literary and romantic fiction. They are worth the money as you will use them frequently.

There is an alternative, free option. Google Fonts are increasingly being used more and more often. Initially created for websites, you can now browse and download their fonts for your own use – they're all royalty-free.

To learn more, head over to *Typefaces: the Good and the (Very) Bad*.

## WORK WITH PROFESSIONAL DESIGN SOFTWARE

Adobe is Queen and ruler of this particular corner of the world. Most designers are taught to use Photoshop, InDesign and the rest of the Creative Suite almost exclusively at college and university. This is why so many processes that require printing, moving image, web-design and advertising use Adobe's applications. They have almost grown with one another.

From a budget perspective, you are looking to spend anything between £10 per month (for a Photoshop and Lightroom combo) to £50 per month for their entire collection.

Obviously, if you're hiring a designer it doesn't matter.

However, if you are planning to try your hand at design (even for marketing) then I would always recommend Adobe – Photoshop and InDesign in particular.

There are more affordable options. Affinity Photo is swiftly becoming a cheaper alternative. It has many of the same features Photoshop has and all for the one-off fee of £48.99 (at time of writing).

Then we have Canva.com. It's another popular choice and, more importantly, free (but you can buy better images for around $1 each). It is limited in terms of effects and style choices, but it is a great starting point for those on a small to zero budget.

## GOOD MARKETING: EVEN THE BEST COVER WILL FAIL WITHOUT HELP

You have spent years thinking about your novel, many more writing it, rewriting it or starting from scratch. You found an editor, an agent or both, who have found every misspelled word and superfluous description. Manuscript finished, you are either searching for a publisher or have found a talented designer to create the perfect cover for your novel. The book is ready, you have a deal or are self-publishing and you are a week away from publication day. This. Is. It.

A week later, excitement and fanfare.

Two weeks after that, things have already cooled off.

Within a month you are wondering what happened.

Simple. You didn't market your book effectively.

I've seen the above happen many times, both in traditional and indie publishing. I've watched well-meaning (and sometimes less than interested) marketing departments and authors create a Twitter profile and think sending fifty updates an hour constitutes a 'marketing campaign'. It doesn't, because you are shouting into a void.

From the very beginning, you should be thinking about

your presence, either online or through the media. There's only one person who will really care about your work, and that's you. Take the initiative, find ways of reaching people and build a fan base.

Here's a list of ways to expand your marketing potential to suit all budgets:

## JOIN A COURSE

I would recommend Mark Dawson's *Advertising for Authors* and *Self-Publishing 101* courses, as I have used both myself. You will learn about the process behind effective campaigns, building a list of readers and using this new fan base to create a strong platform from which to release your novel. Courses such as Mark's have good success rates, especially among those who have followed them fully.

You can learn more about Mark's courses here: selfpublishingformula.com/courses/

## INVEST IN A WEBSITE

Having a simple site with information on your book (or series) and where to buy it, along with your profile, is an important part of building a presence online. Not only because potential readers and fans of your work will be able to find you, it's also a hub of information with which to send people through links and advertisements. A good landing page can mean someone buying your book, signing up to a subscription list and more. Think of it as your business card.

I said 'simple' and I mean simple. A clean design template through Wordpress, Wix, or similar is the most effective; no rotating neon words, no reams of text and no flashing lights. It's all about you and your book.

## FACEBOOK

A Facebook page and group are free platforms to connect with people. You may already have a page but not many likes, but with a bit of work and regular updates (once or twice a week) you can build your followers.

Setting up a group is arguably more important than your page. Since Facebook has updated how and what we see on our walls, group posts have taken priority since January 2018. And videos – live or recorded – will take precedence over text or image.

## TWITTER

Since 2017, Twitter made a few changes to the way they advertise, and it has proven much harder for an author to sell through them. If you prefer Twitter over Facebook – and many do – and feel more comfortable using it, be prepared to work harder.

A good guide to using Twitter is to interact: create conversations, *join* conversations, retweet tweets from people you like and, after a time, they will repay you the favour (honest).

A client of mine, Ian Sutherland, not only writes fantastic thrillers with a cyber-crime twist but is also known for his ability to market using Twitter. He has a bestselling book on the topic called *Advanced Twitter Strategies for Authors* and created Author Platform Sidekick, which is dedicated to helping authors promote themselves using the Twitter platform. Ian was kind enough to offer a few thoughts on the subject:

*'Of all the social media platforms, Twitter is the one that an author has to be seen to be on. And you have to be active, not just relying on a good looking profile page, with minimal actual tweeting. Whenever a reader wishes to engage with an author, Twitter is where they'll go first. A few thousand followers lends credibility to your status as an author, so it's worth following others to attract follow backs. While I recommend regularly posting content, predominantly non-promotional in nature, the minimum level of activity for any author should be to check and respond to mentions at least once a day. After all, it's a social platform. However, all this activity should be considered an investment in building your author brand. No matter how much time you spend on Twitter, it will never become the reason you hit the bestseller lists. So be smart and invest your precious time wisely, focusing your activity on Twitter into daily five or ten minute chunks.'*

## BE ADAPTABLE

If something isn't working, if you're not comfortable talking live to an audience via Facebook, don't give up. Find something you are comfortable with, even if it takes a little while to figure out. You are your books' best hope.

As with most things, a little market research can go a long way. If Twitter and Facebook aren't your thing or you want to branch out onto other social media networks, consider doing a little reading on which social media platforms your readers are most likely using. The Pew Research Center, for example, shares data on the social media platforms Americans use based on age group, gender and even residence. There are many other sources for different markets.

Whatever you do, whether you're traditionally published or doing it yourself, don't rely on others to do it for you. Only use a promotional service if you are 100% sure they are 1) legitimate and 2) don't require you to pay a small fortune to join their list. When it comes to marketing, there isn't a one-size-fits-all way of promoting your book, so a company offering you a service that says it can are either over-exaggerating, doesn't have a clue, or – at worst – lying.

# THE BLURB

How often have you browsed a book store in an airport, searching for that perfect holiday read, and spent most of your time flipping books to their back cover to read the blurb before making a decision? You may have been attracted to the book by its cover, but it was the blurb that sold it.

Having a strong cover is only half the battle. In fact, it is less than half. Your book cover is the ideal first strike – it attracts your potential readers to the book but the cover can only hold their attention for so long.

I asked Bryan Cohen – the book blurb guru – for a more thorough and detailed explanation (which includes a few tips on how to improve your blurb).

*The cover is the ultimate tool to draw readers to your book. Using this artwork on your ads and your social media posts gets browsers onto your Amazon, Kobo, iBooks, or other e-retail sales page. But when these readers reach your page, it always helps to have an ace in the hole. It can make a major difference to give these potential fans something else to love about your book than the cover alone.*

*That's where the book description comes in. To misquote a famous movie, "Copy is your closer." The cover entices readers, the appropriate title and above average reviews keep them on the page, but the words you use to describe your book get them to click the buy button. You could write a whole book on book descriptions (and I have!), but here's what I'd recommend for a copywriting newbie.*

*First, read and study the book descriptions written by the top-selling books in your genre. Take actual notes about what you like and dislike about their copy. Next, write down a few bullet points about your protagonist's journey. You should use this as your basis for the description since no reader will care about your plot synopsis unless there's a compelling character at the centre of it. After you write a rough draft of a description, be willing to rewrite each line as many times as necessary. Even after writing and/or revising over 1,000 descriptions, I'll still need to rewrite some lines 15-20 times to get them right. Lastly, share your description with readers or fellow authors and feel free to include different options for the lines you had trouble with (option A, option B, or option C).*

*This will help you get a start on pairing a compelling description to go with your captivating cover. Good luck!*

Bryan Cohen, BestPageForward.net

# II

## HOW TO WORK WITH A DESIGNER

## DESIGNERS AND WHERE TO FIND THEM

You know what I'm going to say: a good cover is always worth paying for. It is your book's first impression to potential readers and, over time, may even pay for itself.

But let's not remortgage your house just yet. As with all things we purchase, expensive doesn't always bring quality and cheap isn't necessarily inferior. But as a self-published author, especially one who is just starting out, you are no doubt on a budget, and a cover for your novel can often be your greatest expense.

Well just how much should you pay, and what if you can't afford very much at all?

Thankfully there are plenty of options for you, and I'm going to help you make the best choice possible on your budget.

FINDING A DESIGNER

You have apportioned a budget for your cover and have decided you want to commission a designer. There are two options right at the beginning: a designer who has experience designing book covers, and a designer who doesn't. The former is obviously the better choice, but for a new author with a small budget the temptation is usually to look for a bargain.

With that in mind, let's talk about the latter. There are plenty of designers who will happily design a book cover for you. There are even sites that will provide an army of them at your disposal (and maybe below your budget). If you decide to go this route, make sure you research your genre well and write a concise brief beforehand; it will help you get the most out of your designer.

There are obviously pitfalls with this direction, namely worries of quality and experience. Which means there's a chance the project will last longer than anticipated while you go back and forth with feedback or that the final product is substandard.

If you put time and effort into your research and your brief, it should help divert you away from some, if not all, of these pitfalls. You may find a talented designer who is perfect for your needs, and your book is now adorned with a great cover that is rocketing your book up the charts.

Book cover design, along with all design specialities, requires a set of skills that tend to be learned on the job over years of experience; the same can be said again for each genre.

Most freelance book cover designers will have cut their teeth working in-house at a large publishers, and they will likely work for three or more publishers on a regular basis (you will be able to see this on their portfolio site).

A designer with experience in book cover design will be noticeably different to work with and the results tend to be better. However, the freelance world can be harsh for cover designers and publishers often pay well, so be prepared to receive a quote that may be higher than anticipated.

If this is the case but you're desperate to use them, you should mention your maximum budget (if you haven't already) and tell them you understand that a lower cost will mean fewer initial concepts, less design time, and a potentially faster turn around.

Be patient, you may not find a designer within your budget straightaway. They do exist. You just need to keep looking and emailing.

Once you have your designer, head back to the chapter titled *That All Important Brief* so you can get everything prepared to send to them.

**Pro-tip**:

Whatever you do, find your designer way ahead of time. Obviously you need to know what your book is about. Preferably, you have written the first draft at the very least. I would say a minimum of two months before publication would be a good time to start looking. In some cases, six months would be ideal (but that might be pushing it). I receive an email at least once a day asking if we have room in our schedule for a book that has a publishing date in two weeks' time, which is almost always unachievable. Don't leave it to the last minute.

## RECEIVING INITIAL CONCEPTS

You have found your designer and sent them your brief. Now you wait. Having commissioned several cover designers and illustrators, I know how hard this part can be.

Things you will be wondering (and the answers):

- What if my brief wasn't very good? (So long as your designer has all of your information, you will be fine.)
- Are they working on it now? (Probably, some designers are fast and some design everything last-minute. The end results are usually the same.)
- I bet it will be so much better than I thought. (It often is.)
- Will I be disappointed? What if it's rubbish? (Relax, there's always time to make tweaks.)
- Should email them? (Try not to do this unless you have changed an aspect a fundamental aspect of your brief.)

When that moment arrives I want you to remember one thing before you open the attachment:

*A good cover designer will work to a brief, but a great designer will also use their knowledge of your genre and experience to create their own concepts.*

So keep an open mind and let go of that 'perfect' cover you've been developing in your mind since you hit send on that brief (unless your designer is psychic, and they won't be, because, well… that isn't a *thing*).

The ideal process should be: open the file(s), take a quick glance through the designs, move away from your computer, and make a coffee.

Pondering your initial concepts is a bad move. It allows you to ask yourself 'What do I think about this?' Asking yourself this means you are already overthinking. And you will definitely want to share them with friends, fans, or the world via social media. This makes complete sense because you're excited and the responsibility of making a decision – the *right* decision – is difficult.

Just promise me you will hold fire, go make yourself that drink (it can be gin if you want), and come back later.

The reason I say this is because when we are asked, or ask ourselves for our opinion, we start searching for one; even if we didn't have one to begin with. That isn't how we buy books. You need to put yourself in the position of a reader, and that means reacting quickly.

By the time you're back at your computer, you will probably already have a favourite in mind – whether you realise it or not – and you can then look at your concepts properly.

Checklist (grab a pen and piece of paper):

1. Does it meet your brief?
2. If it doesn't meet your brief, are you happy with the concepts?
3. If you are unhappy with your concepts, why?
4. Is everything spelled correctly?
5. Do they fit your genre?
6. If necessary, what tweaks and changes are needed?

## HOW TO GIVE YOUR FEEDBACK IN A NUMBER OF SITUATIONS

**Situation one**: You're happy, no changes.

Well done that designer. Make sure you show your appreciation – design is one of those jobs which is high on criticism and low on praise – and get ready to move to the final stage.

**Situation two**: You're happy, but you would like some changes.

This is probably the standard position. It may not even be down to the concepts. Perhaps you love them but you're not sure about the colours or how the title is sitting.

The best thing you can do is open a dialogue with your designer. Talk to them about what you're thinking and ask them for advice.

As I've mentioned before, pro designers have a huge

amount of experience. This doesn't make them omniscient – and they don't always get things right first time – but they will have reworked enough concepts to know what needs to be done and know how best to meet your requirements.

Whatever you do, don't demand changes or dictate what you think would work best. Even if you've worked in the creative industry before, unless you were a book cover designer, please leave it to the pro. I've had clients send me photos they've found on Google, used Microsoft Paint to make amendments to the design, and even cut the concepts into pieces and glue them back together the way they prefer. I shouldn't have to tell you that this doesn't make for a good client/designer relationship.

**Situation three**: You're unhappy but would like to try again.

This does happen. What you need to do is make sure you know the reason it happened *before* you give your feedback.

1. Were the designs not up to scratch?
2. Did they not meet the right criteria (such as the genre)?
3. Did you hire someone who doesn't work with book covers very often?
4. Or was it your brief? It's okay if it was. It means you can make changes and start fresh.

**Situation four**: You're unhappy and would like to work with another designer.

There are many reasons why you might feel this way. It

can be objective, subjective or even personal. For whatever reason, be sure to be amicable when you part ways.

It is standard to offer a 50% 'kill fee' to your designer, whether you liked their work or not because they still worked on your book. Don't forget to ask yourself (or your designer) what went wrong as you may end up repeating the problem with another designer.

**Situation five**: You've decided to publish at another time, or not at all, and wish to cancel the project.

Life has a way of getting in the way, and we can change our minds. We have all been there, and so has your designer.

If your designer has already sent you several designs, offer a 50% kill fee. The earlier you can let your designer know, the better, and preferably before they have started work. This will also give them time to find a new project to fill your spot.

# COPYRIGHT AND LAYERED FILES:
## WHO OWNS WHAT?

There are two ways to approach the old 'who owns what?' conundrum: the easy way and the more complex way. I'll look at both.

## THE EASY WAY

Unless otherwise stated, the author (that's very likely you) as the client owns the full copyright of the final and approved design work. Simply put, you commissioned the designer to create something that is solely for your use. This isn't always the case when you hire an illustrator (see *The Complex Way* below).

However, this does not include the sole rights of any image (whether photographic or illustrative) or typeface the designer has bought to use as part of the design. This is because the rights belong to the original artist or stock library, and the designer has only bought the right to use them in a design.

The designer has rights too. If you wish to sell on their

...rk to someone else or use their designs for something that wasn't its intended purpose (another product, such as a movie poster, etc.) then you will need their permission. The designer has the right to add the design to their portfolio, too, although if you wish to keep the design hidden for a big 'cover reveal' at a later date then make sure you let them know. Personally, I tend to wait until the cover appears on Amazon.

You can also ask your designer for layered files. They will probably say no, but you can ask to have a version where aspects of the design are not editable (such as the images) with the typography on separate layers.

## THE COMPLEX WAY

The easy way is a broad stroke. It is the 'all smiles' friendly version of how to think about copyright. There can also be subtle differences depending on which country you and the designer are from. So here are a few more in-depth pointers:

- Once you have found your designer, make sure you have confirmation that you, as the client, will have full copyright of the final approved artwork. In the UK, a well-worded email would suffice, but a simple contract would be better. Make sure that you state the work is 'made for hire' and this will tick the US stipulations box too.

- If, for some reason, you don't want your designer to add the design they lovingly created for you in their own portfolio, make sure you tell them up front and have it added to your contract. You may think 'who would do that?' but it does happen, and occasionally for legal or political reasons, but more often than not it's just 'because'.

- Commissioning illustrations is slightly different. You can either agree the work is 'made for hire' or that you have a 'license agreement' to use them. 'Made for hire', as I mention above, means they belong to you and the illustrator/artist can't sell them to another client. However, they may only wish to license their work, which basically means they are not selling the work but selling the right to reproduce the art (and that means they can reuse them wherever they want).

- Earlier I said the designer has rights. They also have 'moral rights' in the UK (as introduced in the UK by the Copyright, Designs and Patents Acts 1988). These cannot be sold or passed on to the client, they remain with the creator even when the copyright doesn't. They include:

1. The Paternity Right: this means the designer has the right to identified as the creator whenever their work is commercially published.
2. The Right of Integrity: basically, you can't use their artwork in a derogatory way.

If you are looking to create your own marketing but are

on a budget, you may want to ask your designer for the layered files so you can do it yourself. More often than not your designer will say no, usually because they don't have the right to give you a file full of copyrighted images they have the sole right to use… but there is a solution.

You can ask your designer for the reference number/name of each image and buy them yourself. This means you have the right of use, too. Obviously, ask your designer first before you purchase anything as you will have wasted your money if they decide not to send you the files.

If you are either confused or worried about copyright, you should Google the rules in both your own and also the designer's country and simply open a dialogue with your designer. Honestly, the easy way is how most of us work. But don't feel you can't ask your designer to sign something as they will, for the most part, be happy to.

III

---

# HOW TO DESIGN A BOOK COVER

# SO YOU WANT TO DESIGN YOUR BOOK COVER?

As exciting as it sounds, deciding to design your own cover is no walk in the park. With that in mind, we need to have a frank discussion about whether this is something you really want to do. Because designing your own book cover is much like DIY in your home. There's a scale of what is possible. If you were a builder before giving it all up to live your dream of writing books, you could probably whip up a conservatory in a weekend.

Alternatively, you may be new to DIY but, with some guidance (like a course) you could successfully tile your kitchen. However, building a house on your own with no experience but a smile and pile of bricks will leave you worse for wear and potentially a little squashed.

I've found authors often fall into one of three categories: nonchalant, cautious or confident. Let's break them apart and look at them in more detail and try to work out which you are:

NONCHALANT

You have no budget and are definitely going to design your own book cover. You don't have a design application but are a whizz in Microsoft Word, and there may be an old version of Paint on your PC. You have an idea and Comic Sans. What more do you need?

Think I'm joking? Google 'Kindle Cover Disasters' and scroll through the Tumblr.

If you are the person I've just described, consider this an intervention. You have already made the right step by buying this book (thank you, by the way), and I want you to know there are plenty of other options.

You can graduate to 'Cautious' by writing a brief for yourself, using 'familiarity theory' to understand your genre and playing with a tool such as Canva (which is free) to create a simple cover. Then, when you have a little more success, you can either invest in a designer, buy a pre-made cover or buy one of the cheaper design applications to play with (see the chapter called *Design Software*).

CAUTIOUS

You could hire a designer, but you are still new to being an author and/or would feel more comfortable trying to create the cover yourself because you have Photoshop (or something similar) and some experience using it. However, you fear you're going to make a mess of it, and what if it doesn't sell?

Fear is a good thing, for the most part. It can be the difference between diving head first into a shallow pool and checking the depth first.

Though it can fill you with anxiety, too. This is where

learning about writing a brief and all the other aspects this book teaches you will come in handy. It is essentially the 'new kitchen' in my forced metaphor earlier: you can do it so long as you have a bit of experience and take guidance.

Once you have control over that fear – because it never goes away, believe me – you will move into the 'Confident' stage.

## CONFIDENT

You are either a designer, have been through my *Self-Publishing Formula Cover Design for Authors* course, were 'Cautious' but have more confidence in yourself, or you are one of those people you meet who are great at everything (like Dave Grohl of Foo Fighters' fame).

By understanding the principles I've set out in this book and combining it with practise and experience, you will have the potential to create book covers that would not look out of place sitting alongside the next Cecilia Ahern. And that is pretty amazing.

# DESIGN SOFTWARE

Once you have decided to design your own book cover, you will have to get to grips with design software. You may have plenty of experience using Photoshop, or be a whizz at Canva, but there is a equally a chance the very thought of using an Adobe product makes your palms sweat. Don't worry. There are plenty of options at various prices and complexities and I will guide you through each of your choices:

## ADOBE PHOTOSHOP AND INDESIGN

Adobe products have ruled the roost for quite some time now, and most designers will have cut their teeth on an Adobe product either at university or in their first job. It is the go-to software for professional designers, photographers, game designers and illustrators.

Photoshop is so well-known and has become such an industry standard, it is now a verb. The image-editing software uses both raster (pixel-based) images and vector graphics, which can be both kept and affected individually using layers (remember that all terms are explained in the *Glossary* at the end of this book).

InDesign is Adobe's desktop publishing software, and it is used predominantly for print-based projects such as magazines, brochures and paperbacks. It can also be used to create ebooks as it exports to EPUB and SWF formats. Many book cover designers will finish their paperback covers in InDesign as the text is vector-based – which means it is crisper – and easier to adapt and format. It also has more options when creating a PDF for output. I should add that it isn't necessary to have InDesign to design your book cover but, if you have it, you should think about using it.

Not too long ago you could purchase each Adobe application separately or as a 'suite' for a one-off fee, but it has since changed to a monthly subscription. Unsurprisingly, this has pushed away a lot of users on a budget or who use Photoshop as an occasional tool – even some freelance designers at the beginning of their careers have had reservations.

The cheapest option is £9.98/$9.99 per month, which includes Photoshop and Lightroom. Lightroom is used to get the most out of your photographs. You will probably never use it, but buying this option is almost £10/$10 cheaper per month than buying Photoshop on its own. You can find it here: www.adobe.com/uk/creativecloud

You may have already bought an older version of Photoshop which, unless it is decades old, will be more than fine to use.

## AFFINITY PHOTO

Created by a team called Serif here in the UK, Affinity Photo is probably the closest you will get to Photoshop without having to pay a monthly fee to Adobe. From editing your images, applying effects and retouching photographs to creating layers, masks and exporting to PDF, Affinity is a great choice for those who have a little more experience in using design software.

I think the biggest pull is its price: a one-off fee of £48.99.

You can learn more and download it here: affinity.serif.com/en-gb/photo/

## GIMP

Don't let the name put you off: it shares very little with *that* scene from *Pulp Fiction*. It actually stands for GNU Image Manipulation Program (where GNU is an operating system comprised of free software).

It has been around in one form or another since 1996 and is a free graphics editor not dissimilar to Photoshop as it can be used for image retouching, editing, free-form drawing and converting between different image formats.

For many pro-designers, GIMP just wasn't up to scratch and lacked features available in Photoshop. However, GIMP is constantly improving and has already become a decent alternative for those on a limited budget.

You can download the most recent version here: www.gimp.org

## CANVA

Canva is a super-simple, drag-and-drop, happy-go-lucky and (mostly) free website dedicated to both web and print media/graphics. It is used by professionals and non-designers for many things, such as flyers, banners, Facebook adverts and even ebooks (you could probably create your paperback, too).

I thought it would be the ideal tool to create tutorials for my Self Publishing Formula module on Facebook advertising, and I've since used it to show how a simple ebook can be created in my *Self Publishing Formula's Cover Design for Authors* course.

Canva obviously has its limitations, which would deter those looking for something much more adaptable and creative. However, it is a great tool for beginners and those who are nervous about using design software or can't yet afford a designer.

Here's a link to the site: www.canva.com

## COLOUR THEORY

Spread over millions of years, tiny genetic mutations in visual pigments allowed us and our eyes to evolve from the rather dim view of the world that our diminutive ancestors had to put up with, into the big ol' apes we are today, who have the whole rainbow to choose from.

Colour has a massive impact on our lives and mood. Not only can they appear warm, cool, bold and soft, they can even affect us in similar ways. They can even have different implications on individual people depending where in the world they're from: red can mean anger and blood here in the UK and Europe, whereas it symbolises happiness and good fortune in China and India.

Of course, most of us know all that. What you really want to know is if we have such a strong bond with colour, why do we find it so bloody difficult to use? Also, why do so many of us choose to wear beige?

Well, I can't help you with the second question (and no one knows the answer to that sartorial conundrum), but I can at least walk you through a few of the design principles surrounding colour and how you should use those principles to help create, define and give your work the right impact. Effectively, colour theory is just another way to help us solve a visual problem, also known as your book cover.

Colour (in art and design) is split into three primary colours, which are then used to create three secondary colours. Finally, we can mix these primary and secondary colours together to produce our six tertiary colours. We call this a 'colour wheel'.

You may find it helpful for this section to google an example of a colour wheel. Don't worry, I can wait.

Found one? Great stuff.

Here's a full rundown...

**Primary colours**:
Red, yellow, and blue.

**Secondary** (which combines the primary colours):
Orange (red + yellow), green (blue + yellow), and violet (red + blue).

**Tertiary** (which combine primary and secondary colours):
Red-orange, yellow-orange, yellow-green, blue-green, blue-violet, and red-violet.

When your working on a project, I would recommend you use a great resource called Adobe Color CC. I have only recently started using it myself. It's great for experimenting with colour theory principles and trying out your palette before and during the design process. You can find it here: color.adobe.com/create/color-wheel

We can use the colour wheel in many different ways, and there are oh-so-many ways. To make it a little simpler, I'm going to show you the three main colour 'harmonies' as I will use them later when talking about cover design.

**Monochromatic**:
One colour used in various shades, using black or white to create darker and lighter colours.

**Analogous**:
Colours that are related to one another on the colour wheel, these make simple and easy combinations. For example, yellow, yellow-orange, and orange.

**Complementary**:
Colours that are opposites on the colour wheel, such as blue and orange. The effect is strong but can be very overpowering and even jarring, which has always made me question the term 'complementary'.


USING COLOURS WITH YOUR BOOK COVER

1. Understanding your genre:

Yes, I'm going to bring up familiarity theory again. If you are a self-published author or new to the design industry, you may have limited knowledge of which colours work well together not only in terms of colour theory, but also within a genre.

For example, the true crime genre is predominantly black, white, and red. It can be any version of this combo, but it does tend to lean towards a black-and-white image with red typography.

Other good examples are thrillers. Shelves are packed with monochromatic covers that often use a strong complementary colour for the typography to make the title leap off the page.

So as you begin to think about your cover, you should look at your research and think of the colour that works well in your genre.

2. Choosing your background colour:

Choosing a background colour is usually the easiest part of the process, and this is your base colour. As I mentioned above, you want to associate your cover with a familiar look within your genre. For example, we associate pastels (pale greens, pinks, and blues) with romantic comedies, red type can mean erotica and green is often seen on sport biographies.

If you decide to use a blue for your thriller, you can adjust the contrast to create a darker more intense image suitable for the psychological end of the genre. Alternatively, you can reduce the saturation just short of grey to produce the more subtle effect consistent with the espionage side of thrillers.

Or if you use a photograph in its natural state for a new adult novel, you can add depth and nuance by tweaking how bright, light, bold, or subtle the colours are.

3. Choosing a colour to support your background:

Obviously, a supporting colour is used to complement or jump out of the background, and it is much less simple.

This is where colour theory is great, especially in terms of colour contrast or harmony.

Say you have chosen a hue of violet as your background for an illustrated contemporary romance cover, you can use an analogous colour palette – in this case it would be violet, blue-violet, and blue – to create a harmonious look with minimal contrast.

However, if you're looking for something much more punchy, you should use a complementary supporting colour. Yellow is opposite on the wheel to violet, so you can add yellow to your cover in the form of type or an added illustrative element to bring vibrancy to your cover.

# TYPEFACES: THE GOOD AND THE (VERY) BAD

For many aspiring designers, the mere whisper of the word 'font' causes them to swoon, but mention 'typeface', and they may end up reaching for a strong drink out of desperation. How do you know which of the thousands of typefaces is the right one to choose? What if *you* think the one you've chosen is perfect, but everyone in the design community thinks it's the worst thing since Comic Sans, and they are laughing at you? Where do you even find a typeface? How much do they cost?

I understand your pain. It can be difficult enough to wrap your head around using the right images, let alone thinking about what the words will look like too.

Don't worry. I will do my very best to walk you through the basics of typography and give you a quick guide to fonts perfect for different genres, both paid-for and free. Oh, and only climate change is worse than Comic Sans.

## THE BASICS

Traditionally, and pedantically, a typeface is a particular design of type – such as Helvetica – and a font is a particular size and weight – like Helvetica Bold. Feel free to use the distinction if you like but don't worry if you use 'font' when you mean 'typeface' because they are pretty much interchangeable these days.

You can break up type into four distinct classifications: Serif, Sans Serif, Script and Decorative. Each of these also have a variety of styles to choose from, and I will give you a quick explanation of each classification, catalogue a few of their styles (including Google Fonts), and tell you the genres to use them with.

## SERIF TYPEFACES

The serif finds its name from the line used at the top and bottom of most letters in this style, kind of like its arms and feet, and it originated in the Latin alphabet with words that were carved into stone during Roman antiquity.

Serifs have long been a firm favourite when setting text because of their readability and appealing curved appearance. When used as your title font, a serif can convey elegance, history, something more literary or a classic mystery. If you scale it larger in size, you will find it works well with cosy mysteries, romance and even psychological thrillers.

**Old Style**: These were the first serifs used in printing. They were created in Italy between the late-fifteenth and mid-eighteenth centuries as an alternative to Gutenberg's blackletter style of print.

**Typefaces include:** Garamond, Palatino, Bembo.
**Google Fonts include:** Cardo, Alegreya, Vollkorn, Gentium Book Basic.
**Perfect for:** general fiction and non-fiction, literary fiction, historical fiction, fantasy.

**Transitional**: Thanks to John Baskerville (during the mid-eighteenth century), transitional serifs are much more refined and often use both slim and thicker strokes. This is due to Baskerville developing and improving both the type of paper used and the method of printing itself.

**Typefaces include:** Baskerville (obviously — the dude invented them, after all), Perpetua, Georgia, Times New Roman.
**Google Fonts include:** Merriweather, PT Serif, Droid Serif, Domine.
**Perfect for:** Classic crime, literary fiction, historical fiction, romance and occasionally children's fiction.

**Modern (or Neoclassical)**: At the time – during the late eighteenth century – these fonts were known as 'modern' as they weren't just updated older styles but altogether new designs. However, since the twentieth century they are often referred to as 'neoclassical'. They pushed the transitional style further and have a strong contrast between thick and thin strokes with square serifs. Think of the font used for *Vogue* magazine as an example.

**Typefaces include:** Bodoni, Walbaum, Didot (the *Vogue* font).

**Google Fonts include:** Playfair Display, Rufina.

**Perfect for:** Romance, crime fiction, literary fiction.


## SANS SERIF TYPEFACES

To put it simply, these are fonts that are without a serif (the feet and arms I waffled on about earlier). Obviously, there's more to it than that. Sans serifs are often much simpler in form than serifs and have less variation in line widths, which means they are perfect for digital displays (as fine serifs can pixellate).

A bold sans serif font used as a title for crime fiction can bring lots of impact, whereas it can give non-fiction a relaxed appeal. A slim and rounded sans serif can create the perfect title for your spy thriller. Add a slight glow to the same font in Photoshop and you have the perfect science fiction title.

**Grotesque**: Not in any way ugly, though it is thought the name originates from the public's first reaction to seeing them, grotesque fonts were the first commercially popular sans serif typefaces due their bold, uniform design which were much more suitable for advertising and headlines.

**Typefaces include:** Trade Gothic, News Gothic, Helvetica, Univers.

**Google Fonts include:** Libre Franklin, Work Sans, Nunitos Sans.

**Perfect for:** Children's fiction, crime fiction, action and adventure, general fiction, non-fiction.

**Geometric**: Using near-perfect circles and squares to build their letter forms, geometric sans serif fonts were super popular in the 1920s and 1930s because of the modern, clean design that worked with the art deco styles of the day. Today we tend to use geometric fonts for titles and subtitles, but rarely smaller text as it can be difficult to read.

**Typefaces include:** Futura, Avenir, ITC Bauhaus.
**Google Fonts include:** Lato, Exo 2, Roboto, Josefin Sans.
**Perfect for:** Spy thrillers, science fiction, crime fiction, literary fiction.

**Humanist**: Not unlike serifs, these fonts have contrast between stroke weight (a letter may be thick in parts and thin in others, like calligraphy). Arguably, these are the easiest to read and the most legible of the sans serif styles, which is why they are used for both display and body text.

**Typefaces include:** Gill Sans, Frutiger, ITC Goudy Sans.
**Google Fonts include:** Cabin, Open Sans, Raleway.
**Perfect for:** General fiction and non-fiction, crime fiction, cookery, young adult, romance, science fiction.

SCRIPT TYPEFACES:

As the name suggests, script typefaces are based on – sometimes literally – the strokes created in handwriting. They can have a more regular, consistent shape or be much looser and more casual. Either way, they are far too complex for body type and almost always used for titles.

A more formal script can bring an air of sophistication to

a classic such as *Pride and Prejudice* or a sense of whimsy to a romantic comedy. A looser script can denote historical non-fiction or even literary fiction.

Tip: Never use a script typeface in all-caps. It will make for difficult reading and genuinely looks bad.

**Formal**: Created using seventeenth-century handwriting styles, the majority of which were based on writers such as George Shelly, these fonts have clean lines that reflect the thin and thick strokes of a quill. Formal script fonts are elegant and can create a sophisticated tone and wonderful initials.

**Typefaces include:** Bickham Script, Young Baroque, Snell Roundhand.
**Google Fonts include:** Pinyon Script, Cookie, Petit Formal Script.
**Perfect for:** historical fiction and non-fiction, romantic fiction, fantasy, classic fiction.

**Casual**: Designed with a less formal and more friendly design in mind, the letters can vary in size and width as if written quickly with a brush (rather than a quill). Casual fonts were huge in the 1970s in North America as well as Europe and used heavily in advertising, but they are often used today for a more intimate and informal look.

**Typefaces include:** Freestyle Script, Brush Up, Claudia, Boulevard.
**Google Fonts include:** Pacifico, Dancing Script, Yellowtail.

**Perfect for:** Romantic comedy, literary fiction, young adult, children's fiction, fantasy.

## DECORATIVE TYPEFACES

Pretty much everything else falls under this category as it is so diverse. Used for signage, headlines, and anything that needs a strong typographic style, decorative fonts are frequently associated with a time period, theme or even an aspect of culture – such as graffiti, grunge, cartoons or military styles.

As much as they are popular, they are also time-sensitive and can be abandoned when they go out of fashion, so be careful when picking a decorative typeface.

Due to their sheer variety and volume, these fonts don't have subsections – as they would go on forever – but I will suggest a selection of popular ones.

**Typefaces include:** Frontage Condensed, Lumiere, Veneer, Town, Montecatini, Ponche Bourbon.
**Google Fonts include:** Lobster, Righteous, Bangers, Special Elite.
**Perfect for**: non-fiction, cookery, young adult, science fiction, children's fiction, fantasy and even crime — most genres, really.

## THE TYPEFACES TO STEER CLEAR OF

I was once told that there is no such thing as a bad typeface, just bad ways of using them. This was of course complete nonsense (and I no longer speak to that person). That sentiment definitely works with standard typefaces, but that is usually just a poor choice rather than a bad typeface.

Bad typefaces are like killers in a 1980s horror movie: they don't care whether you are rich or poor, appear out of nowhere when you are at your weakest and have already escaped from your font library more than once. They just won't die.

A quick way to assess whether the font you are using is in fact one of these bad fonts is if any of the following apply:

1. You have seen it used in your boss's PowerPoint presentations.
2. Your church used it on a flyer to advertise their jumble sale.
3. Your neighbour used it on a poster for their missing cat.
4. It came with your PC (this is especially true of decorative and script fonts).
5. It looks like balloons.
6. You think it looks 'cute'.

We all know Comic Sans ticks all of these boxes. Other offenders include:

- Brush Script
- Papyrus
- Curlz
- Any font with the word 'Hand' after it (such as Bradley Hand)
- Mistral
- Stencil

There are many more. Lots of them would fall under the category of a decorative typeface, so they may slip by.

In all honesty, it's not that these typefaces are bad or ugly (well, some are). It's about their bad associations (like the list above). They almost always come from the standard list of fonts found on your PC, they look 'fun' and have been used a billion times already (and that's just by your mum).

# YOUR BRAND

Whether you are an author of a series who is taking the design reins at book six, or you have written book one of a six-book collection, it is worth considering how your series will look ahead of time. From the style and colours of the image to your name and title placement, you should think about how all of these design aspects will carry across your series of covers.

The decisions you make on your first design will affect everything else, and the solutions are very simple and almost always overlooked (even by pros).

## COLOURS

A great way to distinguish between the individual books in your series and emphasise your brand is to use a different colour for each of your books on the same aspect of the cover, i.e., title, author name, spine block, or even the background colour. This only becomes an issue when you run out of colours.

A good example is Stephen King's extensive backlist in the UK. Each have the same design-style and use colour to distinguish them. However, due to the sheer number of titles (52 at the time), picking a different colour per book would – and did – drive me insane. In the end, we came up with the idea to separate King's books into a series of categories (Chillers, Iconic and so on) so that we could give each set a colour.

If you're planning on keeping the same colour scheme throughout the series, think about how readers will differentiate between them. Yeah, the title is different, but it's usually not enough.

## TITLE LENGTH AND SIZE

This affects so many authors of a series. Book one has the short and punchy title of 'War'. The design decision is to make it big and bold, from edge to edge, and build your composition around it. You publish... then struggle with book two's title 'The Aftermath'.

It's not always possible to know the title of your next book but keep in mind that whatever you decide for your first design will have to work on the rest of your series.

## REPEATING IMAGES OR MOTIFS

This is especially prevalent in non-fiction as repeating something as simple as a logo, illustration, or even repeating parts of your title in the exact same style and layout can really help build your brand recognition.

To a lesser extent, it can also work across some styles of

action thriller and romance. Using the same image, say a running figure or an illustrated motif like a heart, across your covers is a decent way to create association with your series (especially if you're on a budget) but only if you differentiate in some way. Colours are the simplest way to do this, having a different scene and background can help too (especially with your running figure).

## REFRESHING YOUR BACKLIST

This can be as simple as tidying up and adding uniformity across your previous covers. You don't even have to change the images — just add new typography and make sure the aesthetic works throughout. Or you can start afresh by giving your latest book a whole new style and then reworking the previous books in the series to match.

## HOW TO FORM A CONCEPT FROM
## YOUR BRIEF

Many think the genesis of design is 'a good idea', as if it is hanging around in the back of your mind like a sweaty contestant on *The Voice* waiting for its turn in the spotlight. This may be the truth for artists, but this isn't the truth for many designers (myself included). We can't know what we're going to create until we know what we're designing. We need a brief.

To continue the terrible analogy above, the brief is the stage, it is the competition itself. It is the framework on which an idea is built, and it is where all of your information will be found, from title and genre to synopsis and character descriptions.

As you are creating your own cover, I recommend that you write one for yourself which, luckily for you, I have already written about in the chapter *That All Important Brief.* I would recommend rereading the chapter on *Familiarity Theory,* too. It will aid you in your understanding of both your genre and your market.

Once you have written your brief and researched your

comparative and competitive book cover visuals, now is the time to create an idea.

Designers are, at their very core, problem solvers. So you should think of your book cover as a conundrum for which you need a solution. Writing a brief is the best way to present that problem as it contains all of the salient information, which in turn allows you to create solutions to the problem: and these are your concepts.

Your concept(s) will lead to choices in image, colour, typography, aesthetic and can help determine a style for your series (should you have one).

## WE CAN BUILD CONCEPTS USING THREE STAGES

**Narrative** – places, character descriptions, important objects or scenes. This is your concept in its most basic form and can be a great starting point for picture research.

**Tone** – descriptive words, mood, comparative book covers, picture research and illustration styles. The tone of an early concept is often abstract, but it gives the narrative substance.

**Composition** – sketches, choices of typography, style and placement of imagery along with colour choices and how they all work together. These hold the narrative and visual elements of your concept together.

The best way to show you is to walk you through a quick and simple project.

The synopsis: *It's an urban fantasy novel with a female protagonist set in New York.*

To begin, we focus on narrative. In this case we can make notes on what the female protagonist looks like, where in New York the action or some of the scenes are set (and remember not to restrain yourself with literal interpretations) and read through the synopsis to get an idea of her character.

Armed with this information, we can begin to breathe life into the concept by using tone. As I mentioned above, tone is often abstract as it refers to what you want your cover to convey rather than how it will look. This is helpful, believe it or not, as it can help sharpen our minds to an aesthetic style before we've started picture researching.

In terms of our brief, we could use words such as *strength*, *apocalypse*, *urban*, *grunge*, *bold*, *bright* etc. What do you want your cover to say?

Before you start trawling through images looking for photographs of our heroine and wide-angle shots of Times Square, take a look through your comparative cover research to see how your models should be positioned and the styles of imagery that work best. This will help you choose the right image when you begin researching. (You can find more information in the chapter *Picture Research*).

Finally, we can start putting some meat on those bare bones of a concept by working on your composition. Step away from the computer and grab a pen or pencil and some paper too. It might feel antiquated these days, but a basic sketch of your book cover – even if it looks like an incoherent mess – can really help create a much clearer objective before working it up digitally. This is especially the case when used in conjunction with your comparative book cover research as it enables you to plot where your character should go and how they interact with their background. It also lets you determine how to prioritise your typography (author name size, whether title or name should come first, etc.) and allows you to play about with additional flourishes such as quotes, subtitles or even roundels. If you are new to cover design I would recommend that you adhere as closely as you can to the compositions used in your genre – from character positioning to font choice and style – as it will make this process much easier.

Once you are ready, start turning your concept into your design digitally using your software to manipulate the images and typography you have chosen.

You will likely develop a preference, such as sketching out concepts without needing a visual or tonal cue. Or perhaps you will jump straight in to picture research as it helps to spark an idea. However you do it, and so long as you do your research and understand your genre, you will solve the problem.

After a time, a concept may pop into your head as you read your brief – and I don't mean in some hippy, Jedi Master way. It can be as simple as a font choice and as complex as the interplay between a character and background (though it doesn't always make it to the final design). These are the initial stages of your subconscious starting down a now-well-trodden path to your concept before you, and it's pretty exciting when it happens.

# PICTURE RESEARCH

You have written your brief and filled it with characters, places and other important details, alongside which you will find a comparative cover or two. Hopefully you have an idea swimming around your head, and you are ready to design. But first you need to find the right images.

Trawling through hundreds or thousands of awful images to find something that bears some resemblance to what you are looking for – also known as 'picture research' – is without doubt the most time consuming aspect of commercial book cover design.

Seasoned designers who have journeyed the well-trodden, yet ridiculously steep and tiresome, path to find the right images will often have a good idea of what they're looking for and how to find it way before they have even embarked on the journey. Fear not, I'm going to help you to (hopefully) shorten your quest for images.

Before I do, let's discuss the differences between royalty-free and rights-managed images as I will mention each term a few times throughout.

**Royalty-free** simply means you can freely use an image repeatedly after initial purchase without paying any additional royalties. So you still have to purchase the image but it is usually a one-off fee. How often you can use the image depends on where you have bought it. For example, Shutterstock has a limit of 500,000 uses on a single royalty-free image – and uses include every printed copy of your paperback (but not your ebook, as it is digital).

You also do not own the image you have bought; you merely have the rights to use that image without any further fees or interruption from the copyright owner (unless you break the terms, of course).

**Rights-managed** allows you to effectively 'rent' an image exclusively for a specified time, territory and even use, such as a book cover. It also offers the ability to restrict anybody else from using the image for similar content. Bear in mind that you can't reuse this image on anything other than the intended purpose you bought it for, which means you can use it in marketing for your book but not on a new book with a different title.

As an example, the cost of a rights-managed photograph from Getty Images will depend on the size you require, the countries you wish to sell it in (known as territories), the amount you intend to print and the duration for which you wish to use the image. The exclusive rights to a full-page image with a print run of five thousand sold worldwide for five years could burn a £1,325/$1,760 hole in your pocket.

Many stock image libraries offer a mixture of both. Those of a higher quality will have fewer or possibly no royalty-free options.

There are a number of stock image sites to suit a variety of budgets and, as with many things, the price of a product doesn't always equate to its quality. You may even find the same photographs and illustrations available through other sites at a cheaper price. It is always worth having a shop around. Here are a few for you to browse with an idea of costs.

**Larger Budget**

Getty Images:

Known for creating and selling award-winning rights-managed and editorial photography (and you will often see their name alongside photographs in newspapers and magazines), Getty also have a large range of royalty-free images.

From their main site (see iStock below for Getty's more affordable option), the same royalty-free image can cost anything from £50/$65 to £485/$640 depending on the size and resolution you require.

Arcangel Images:

Arguably the best stock image site for commercial fiction, especially crime and thriller, with work that has adorned many book covers since they began in 2004. Their aim is to supply clients with the type of images previously only available through commission, which essentially means their photography rocks.

They offer both royalty-free (priced from £49 to £299 per image) and rights-managed.

Trevillion Images:

Another library filled with beautiful photography, Trevillion has a premium collection of photography sourced from some of the best artists across the world and includes anything from fantasy to romance.

They don't have a royalty-free option, but they try to be flexible and competitive with their rights-managed fees... but you will need to request a quote if you like an image.

**Smaller Budget**

Shutterstock:

There is rarely a day that I'm not searching Shutterstock for an image, which is honestly a shock to me as there was a time when it was like digging up a beach to find a diamond. Yet they have become my stock library of choice and have swiftly become traditional publishing's favourite, too. This is due to a decent mixture of quality and price, which makes it a great choice for self-published authors.

You can buy a month-to-month or annual subscription, and can pay anything between £29 for 10 images to £149 for 750 images.

As with all royalty-free libraries, you can still spend a long time searching what you need, but I've found a few diamonds.

123RF:

Yes I know, it doesn't sound like a 'real' website and no, you won't get hacked. 123RF are very similar to Shutterstock in terms of image choice and quality, but you sometimes have to do a little more digging.

That said, their pricing plans are definitely value for money. A monthly subscription of 150 images is only £59, but it does come with a download limit of five images per day.

Creative Market:

They aren't technically a stock image site – although they do have royalty-free images – but I have added them to the list because they are becoming one of my most-used resources for typefaces, illustrations, Photoshop effects and even website templates for authors.

You can buy an individual image or typeface for as little as $9, or use their pro service and buy a monthly subscription for between $49 to $199 (depending on how much and how often you want to download).

iStock:

This is Getty Images' more affordable option. They have two royalty-free collections, Essentials and Signature, which mean 'cheaper' and 'more expensive' respectively.

There are a few price options: you can either buy an image directly, pay for credits or buy a monthly or annual subscription.

Free image sites:

Be careful when using free image sites, such as Pixels and Pixabay, as they present their images as available for commercial purposes but more often than not the photographers posting the images didn't necessarily get a release from the model to use their likeness. In general, it is better to avoid using images with people unless the image explicitly states they have obtained a model release. In a similar vein, it is a good idea to do a quick reverse-image search with TinEye.com or Google Reverse Image Search to ensure that the image has not been lifted from a photographer's website or the like.

Generally speaking, it is better to go with an inexpensive stock site than risk the liability that comes with using a free image site.

## KEYWORDS

When you are picture researching, you are generally searching for three things: people, places and objects. Each requires a slightly different combination of keywords, and some are far easier than others. Also, looking for the perfect image – your slovenly detective strolling towards a murder scene in a dark alley in Chicago – is almost impossible, and it will make the task much easier if you search for each image separately.

Let's begin…

Take one of the settings of your novel: There is a big scene in London, and your idea is to show your character racing on foot at night from Point A to the Palace of Westminster. Searching for *'London'* alone will generate a lot of images from different perspectives. You have a destination, so you could try *'Palace of Westminster'*, *'Houses of Parliament'* or simply *'Big Ben'*. This will bring better results, but you will still have a lot of images in different styles and angles.

Defining is the key to keywords. For the example above, searching for *'Big Ben Road Night'* will usually start you off in the right direction (and you will still have to scroll through loads of images, obviously).

So you have your scene, let's find your character.

Your protagonist is an ex-assassin who is making up for her dark past by doing good, and in which case you need a photograph of a running woman. Searching for *'running woman'* will present you with thousands of women jogging or racing in the Olympics, but it's rarely what you're looking for. You need to change those words a little bit. Stick with *'woman'* and add *'walking away'* or *'woman action running away'*.

I realise this may feel like I'm trying to explain to you how to write your own name, but it's an area many get stuck on and, when faced with a page full of images, it can be hard to find what you're looking for.

Another example, perhaps for a psychological thriller. You could search for *'scared man'* but what you might find is a whole host of horror images. Whereas *'man face shadow'* would produce better results. You need to define your keywords and remember that there is no need to be overly specific.

The final example is for a romance set in the summer, and these tend to have an illustrated style so adding the term *'illustration'* is a good start (some stock libraries will have an option to search only for illustrations). If the setting is the beach, think about the type of beach: is it the seaside or a tropical getaway? Searching for a *'woman summer'* may be too broad, but a small change to *'woman summer sunglasses'* will bring better results.

**Pro-tip**:

Test your images before you buy them. If you are worried your chosen images won't work together you can try them out for free by downloading them straight to your computer by right-clicking the image in your browser and saving. It may have watermarks across it, and it will definitely be very low-resolution, but it's a great way to test the images before you buy them. Then, once you're happy with the layout and how everything looks together, you can buy the high-resolution images and swap them in.

**Warning**: don't work with low-resolution images on your concept for too long (adding effects, etc.) as it will mean redoing all of your artwork all over again once you have bought the high-resolution images.

# DESIGN TIPS TO GET YOU STARTED

## TYPOGRAPHY HIERARCHY

Depending on your genre – and style within your genre – your front cover typography will need to sit within a defined hierarchy.

*Why is that, Stu? Surely it's simply title and author?*

You would think so, but it's much more detailed than that. Imagine having all of your text in capital letters and in a large size. All that will do is throw everything at you at once. It is the typographic equivalent of shouting in your face.

What you want your cover to do is deliver the right information in the right sequence, and there are a number of ways of doing this.

**Uppercase and titlecase:** If your genre tends to have a large title or author name entirely in uppercase, you can create focus and reduce noise by keeping the rest of the text smaller and in titlecase.

**Text size:** Try not to use text of a similar size or weight on your cover. For instance, your title is large but lacking impact on your cover. Try reducing the size or weight of the author name and surrounding text. This will bring more emphasis to your title.

**Never an afterthought:** When designing your cover, always consider where your type will go. I often see titles squeezed in a small space of sky, or the author name and quote squashed together like a type-sandwich. Your typography is part of your design, not just your image.

**Clean and simple:** When choosing your typefaces try to stick to two styles maximum. Too many styles will create noise and make it difficult to read. And never use more than one decorative font at the same time.

**Colours:** A simple way to bring hierarchy into your typography is to use colour. Using a vibrant colour on your primary type (such as your title) can make it pop, and changing your secondary type to analogous colour gives the primary type a subtle nudge forward.

So long as you are following your genre rules (see the chapter on *Familiarity Theory*) you will be fine. And remember not to shout.

NEGATIVE SPACE

Negative space is the empty space which defines an object or typographic element. The more space they have, the more defined they become, and you can even break them into sections or create a hierarchy which becomes easier to process.

Think of negative space as the branches on a tree. Each branch is defined by the light which surrounds it and passes through it. The more branches there are, the less light there is and the more complex the area becomes. If we cut back some of those branches, we begin to see individual definition.

When we fill our designs with text (such as long quotes and subtitles) it will become difficult to focus on what is important as the text is forcing your title and image to compete for attention.

The same can happen with images. The more complicated we make a scene for our protagonist, the harder it will be to spot them.

## SIMPLE DESIGN

Whether you are new to design or have experience, a good tip is to keep your design simple. In some cases, you may not need more than one image and one typeface to create the perfect cover for your genre.

Here are a few pointers to help keep your designs simple and effective:

**Colour:** Keep you palette to a minimum and research what works best within your genre. If you're working on a thriller cover, a bright yellow will pop against dark blue, but throw in red or green and you will have chaos.

**Focal point:** Using your character, place or object as a focal point can mean you are less likely to need bold typography to send your message. A great example of this is the UK edition of *Before I Go to Sleep*. All it needed was a close-up of the character's eye. Young Adult fiction does this a lot too, but rather than characters they use a single logo, such as with *The Hunger Games*.

**Fewer type styles:** It goes without saying, really. But using one type style (two maximum) will keep your message clear. A script serif for your title goes very well with a simple serif for the rest of your text. Using a different style of serif for each aspect (such as your author and subtitle) will create too much complexity.

**Alignment:** Try not to align your type in different directions. If your title is centred, so should be the rest of your text. The only time you can break this rule is if you have a quote or roundel (this is text contained within a circle) which needs to float in an empty space away from the main area of text.

# MYTH-BUSTING

Whether sitting in a book cover meeting with publishers and sales execs or reading comments on an indie author Facebook group, I often hear the same myths about cover design being used as truths. So I thought I would do you the honour of popping the bubble of a few of the most famous of untruths.

## NOBODY BUYS GREEN BOOKS

I have heard this my entire career. You can swap green for brown and, less frequently, blue.

Not only are the majority of books on sports green, but many bestselling contemporary romance and sci-fi novels use tones of green too.

## ONLY BESTSELLING AUTHORS HAVE LARGE NAMES

This is what people say when they think, often wrongly, that you are too big for your boots. *How dare you!* they shout. *Only Lee Child has been afforded that privilege.*

It's piffle, as you know.

If your genre has a plethora of authors with their names on two lines, with the title coming in second-place, then feel free to emulate that style. The same works the opposite direction: if your genre tends to have the name on a single line, then you should follow that style instead.

## EVERYTHING MUST BE LEGIBLE AS A THUMBNAIL

I was a junior designer when Kindle-fever took hold. It felt like every marketing director and editor had lost their minds overnight, screaming about thumbnails like there had been a mishap with a hammer. Suddenly we could not sell a book unless the title and author name were ten times the size they originally were.

What they had seemingly forgotten was we had been selling books on Amazon using thumbnails, without any problems, for years.

Not unlike the book you spot from across the store, you won't truly know what the book is about until you read the blurb. And that is the same for online stores, too. So don't worry about everything being legible. Care about how your cover looks and how your blurb reads.

## WHITE COVERS DON'T WORK ON AMAZON

This is myth that was born of the concern authors, sales execs and editors had when the saw the thumbnail online and worried no one would be able to see it. I completely understand the concern too, but it's similar to the legibility myth in that it has absolutely no basis in truth.

Another myth about white covers is that they give some people an uneasy feeling that buyers will think the design is unfinished, or they fear the amount of open space. So long as the design works, that is all that really matters.

## PEOPLE CAN'T READ HORIZONTAL TYPE

Out of all of the many myths on book design, *'People aren't able to read type horizontally'* makes me laugh and roll my eyes the most, simply because mere inches away both the title and author name are written horizontally along the spine (and have been for many, many, years).

## IV

EBOOKS, PAPERBACKS
AND SPINES... OH MY!

# BEFORE YOU BEGIN

Setting up your initial file and preparing it for print is easy, especially if you are designing for ebook only. The most complex part is deciding your trim size and knowing who you are printing or selling through, as each have their own requirements. Even using the same information for your paperback (format and page count) can create a slightly different spine width. However, before we start we need to have a quick chat about the basics of creating a document for design.

## COLOUR MODES

It is essential that you know which mode to use before you start designing. We predominantly use two modes of colour in design, RGB and CMYK, and each have their pros and cons.

RGB: this mode uses the primary colours of **red**, **green,** and **blue** to form pretty much every colour you can imagine. It is used as a colour mode for most screens, from your monitor to your phone, and for any image you find on the internet. This will be the colour mode of your ebook cover.

CMYK: this mode uses **cyan**, **magenta**, **yellow,** and **key**. Yep, 'key' isn't a colour; it means black.

Even though it has four colours, it doesn't have the depth or variety of colours RGB has on offer. This is especially true when it comes to super bright colours like neon pinks, blues, and greens. You can still create artwork filled with colours, but you have fewer options.

Bear in mind that CMYK is used as the main colour mode by pretty much every printing company across the world and will therefore be your choice for paperback.

*So, RGB for ebook and CMYK for paperback you say?*

Technically yes… but no. I would always recommend you design in CMYK regardless because you will save yourself a lot of heartache (and headaches) when the colours on the cover you have spent so long working on become muted after conversion from RGB to CMYK.

Converting the opposite way – from CMYK to RGB – will not cause this problem, so once you have your final flattened cover and need to create your ebook you can simple change the modes without issue.

## YOUR DOCUMENT RESOLUTION (DPI)

If you have ever worked with a designer or needed printed materials before, it is likely you will have come across the term dpi and ppi. They stand for 'Dots Per Inch' and 'Pixels Per Inch', respectively. They are exactly the same thing, so going forward I will just call it dpi.

Dpi is usually preceded by a number that represents how many dots per inch you have in a printed document. The higher the number of dots, the clearer and better quality the final print will be (though there is a ceiling on that number, and I'll explain more below).

You may also have heard the terms 'high-resolution/hi-res' and 'low-resolution/low-res', and these are directly related to the amount of dpi your image has. Try not to confuse these terms with quality. A low-resolution image may not be good enough for a printed document but would be perfect for a visual on your website.

When designing and printing relatively small things like books (or birthday cards, posters etc), we use 300dpi. 300 dots per inch is pretty much the limit as there is no discernible difference should you up the number and it would just be a waste of ink.

So when you come to setting up your file using your trim size (see the chapter titled *Creating Your Paperback*), make sure it is 300dpi.

# CREATING YOUR PAPERBACK

Whether you are using CreateSpace, KDP Print or Ingram Spark, you will need to choose your trim size before you begin the design process. There are no strict rules to adhere to as there are a variety to choose from, and the only real difference will be the size and thickness of your book. For example, choosing the smallest size of 4 inches by 6 inches (4" x 6") will produce a larger spine than 7 inches by 10 inches (7" x 10"). This is obvious, I know, but it's worth saying so you don't forget about it.

The majority of my clients use 5" x 8" as their trim size, mostly because it is the same size as the paperbacks you will buy online or in stores. The next in terms of popularity are 5.25" x 8" and 5.5" x 8.5"; I rarely have to design anything larger or smaller. If you have always preferred a trade paperback over a standard paperback – they are basically a hardback without the board and jacket – then the closest trim size would be 6" x 9".

Once you know your trim size, you can create a template using your chosen publishing resource. The most important information you will need is your book's final formatted page count (not your standard A4 manuscript; it needs to be formatted to your trim size) to create the template, and each company requires slightly more or less information but they are essentially the same in terms of their processes (links to the individual companies are below).

- **Interior type**: Black and White or Full Colour – essentially how the interior of your book will look. Your standard novel will be black and white, whereas some non-fiction is in full colour and will require different paper.
- **Trim size**: The width and height of your book.
- **Number of pages**: Fairly obvious, but do make sure you use your final formatted page count (including copyright page, table of contents and similar additions) or else your spine width will not be accurate.
- **Paper colour**: White or cream – many of my clients go for cream, perhaps because white is often associated with non-fiction. Either way, the choice is yours. The only difference this decision will make will be on the spine width as each coloured paper will be ever so slightly different in thickness.

Once you have entered all of your information you can create your template. This will be presented as either a downloadable file or emailed to you. There may be additional options for each company, and I've added those in the next chapter along with the links.

**Please note**: If you are printing through both Ingram Spark and CreateSpace, you will need to create a template for both. Even with the same information, the spine width may vary ever so slightly, and this is due to different weights of paper and varying printing processes.

Your template will give you all the information you need to create your paperback cover. Here's a quick guide to all the terms you will need to know:

- **Trim size**: You should probably know this as you chose it, but this will now include both your spine width and your back cover.
- **Bleed**: A bleed is essentially an extension of your trim size, and your image should extend to meet it. This is to limit mistakes during the (not always accurate) trimming process. Say your image fits your trim size exactly, so if the printer cuts too far outside of that, your book will have a white line or border. The standard bleed size is 0.125 inches on all sides.
- **Live/Safe area**: Your template will likely give you a guide to where your important information should go and not extend beyond, such as your text, logos, and barcode. If they extend beyond this area they may get trimmed.
- **Spine**: Your spine width will be unique to the

book and based on the information you gave (see above). The spine area will have similar guides and rules to the live/safe areas to ensure your text and images don't overlap onto your front and back covers.

Each company will display their template a little differently. For example, CreateSpace and KDP Print (which are basically the same) will send you a file that meets the exact trim and bleed of your cover, but IngramSpark will send a larger page with your template sitting top right.

In all cases, the back cover will be displayed to the left, the spine centre, and the front cover will be on the right of the spine.

# WHAT DO I DO NEXT?

Whether you are using Photoshop or one of the other programs I mentioned in the chapter on *Design Software*, you will need to start by creating a file using the full trim size including the bleed. All of that information is on your template, but in case it isn't clear here is an example:

Your trim size is 5" width by 8" height. This will be the same for your front and back covers. Your spine width has been calculated as 0.75", and your bleed will be the standard 0.125" on all sides (which is a total of 0.25" added to the width and height). The trim height won't change, but the width will. Here's how to calculate it using our details:

5" (back) + 0.75" (spine) + 5" (front) = 10.75" width

Now we need to add the bleed to the width and height, which is simple a case of adding 0.25 to each (0.125 on each side, remember?). In this case, the height will be:

8" + 0.25" = 8.25" and the width is 10.75" +
0.25" = 11".

Our final trim size including bleed will be 11" x 8.25".

You can use guides within your design software to mark
out where the bleed and spine should go.

**Tip for first-time designers**: If you are using Photoshop,
you can work straight on top of your template. All you need
to do is open the file and build your artwork on top. This
would be a great route to take if you are very new to
designing your book covers as it will limit many mistakes.

You can download your templates and more information
here:

CreateSpace: www.createspace.com/Help/Book/Artwork.do

KDP: kdp.amazon.com/en_US/cover-templates

IngramSpark:
myaccount.ingramspark.com/Portal/Tools/CoverTemplateGe
nerator

**Quick note**: IngramSpark will ask for your ISBN along with
the rest of your information in building your template, and
that means you can take into account the positioning of your
design around the box.

If you own a copy of InDesign (Adobe's publishing

software), you have the option of downloading an InDesign template to work with, which will give you more control over the final design.

# PREPARING YOUR PAPERBACK
## FOR PRINT

Once you have finished your paperback and triple-checked that your guides, bleed, and images are all in the right places, you will need to output the final file for print. Every piece of design software is a little different. In some cases it is as easy as using the 'Print' command.

Your chosen publishing resource will have guidelines on how they prefer to receive their files, but essentially it is either a PDF (Portable Document Format) or a jpeg. The requirements can, and have, changed over the years, so I won't go into this in great the detail and would highly recommend reading the guidelines CreateSpace *et al* provide.

That said, here is a basic outline so you are familiar with the process:

- You can use the 'Save As', 'Export', and/or 'Print' commands (depending on your design software). In this case, we will use 'Print'.
- Once the dialogue box opens, you can either

select PDF from the choice of printers available or there may be a 'Print to PDF' option.

- You will need to choose 'PDF/X-1a' as your setting; you can find this under 'Properties', 'Settings' or 'Options' depending on your software and PC.
- Once you click 'OK' and select where the file should be saved, you have your PDF ready to upload.

**Pro-tip**:

When using Photoshop, be sure to save often. Also, when you are ready to produce your ebook and paperback, create a duplicate document so as not to accidentally save over your work.

# CREATING YOUR EBOOK

There are two ways to accomplish this. The first is only relevant if you have already created a paperback. All you need to do is crop the front cover, change the mode to RGB and save the new file as a jpeg, and you have your ebook cover.

The second way is very similar to creating a paperback. You choose a trim size and create your cover (although, in this case, the ebook will not need to be 'trimmed'). An ebook-only design is measured in pixels (aka 'px') rather than inches as it is for digital purposes and should be designed in RGB, where the standard dimensions are 1563px wide by 2500px high. You can check with CreateSpace and the others regarding what they would prefer before you start.

However, I recommend that you choose one of the print trim sizes (such as 5" x 8"). The reason for this is simple: you may want to have a paperback version one day, which will require you to 1) change your artwork to fit your trim size and 2) you will have to deal with the fallout of RGB to CMYK conversion problems. Even if you are 99% sure you will never have need for a paperback, do it anyway. Pretend I never told you about ebook dimensions or pixels if it helps.

If you follow my recommendation, this is what you should do:

- Choose your trim size (there is no need to create a template; you only need to know the front cover dimensions).
- Add your bleed, even though you will never need it for your ebook it will prove invaluable when or if you ever need to create a paperback as you will have extra image to work with.
- Design your cover as normal.
- When finished, duplicate your document and crop your artwork to your trim size.
- Convert the file to RGB.
- You can either save as a jpeg or create a PDF using the technique in *Preparing your paperback for print* (just above).

**Pro-tip**:

If you decide to use a print trim size for your ebook cover, make sure the pixel height is 2500px or higher. You can check and change this in Photoshop by selecting 'Image' and 'Image Size'.

# SO LONG, AND THANKS FOR ALL THE FONTS.

I have spent a long time thinking about this book, about how it would take shape and how best to make it useful to both authors and designers alike. It was important for me to impart what was informative and effective rather than write a 'one size fits all' book which merely stated a few facts but had no substance.

Everything slotted into place during my time creating *Self-Publishing Formula's Cover Design for Authors* course, because I had to really define the processes I've used on a daily basis and turn them into something almost tangible. The practical tutorials I created had to also explain the theory behind what I was doing, otherwise our students wouldn't learn why one design aspect worked over another.

Once the students started using the course and were creating wonderful designs of their own, I knew I could explain the process in such a way as for it to be effective. And so I finally started writing this book.

I hope you have found the guide useful. If you enjoyed the book and are looking for a more practical guide you should definitely look into my online course as it will build on what you have already learned. You can find the course here: selfpublishingformula.com/design

Thank you for reading,

Stuart Bache

**Enjoy this book? You can make a big difference.**

Reviews are one of the most powerful marketing tools an author has, and honest reviews can help bring this book to the attention of other authors whose book sales would benefit from stronger, more professional covers.

If you have enjoyed this book and found it helpful, I would be very grateful if you could spend a few minutes leaving a short review on my book's Amazon page.

Thank you very much.

Stuart

# GLOSSARY

**Adobe:** An American multinational computer software company focused on the creation of multimedia and creativity software products. Best know for Photoshop, Acrobat Reader (for reading PDF documents) and Adobe Creative Cloud.

**Artwork:** Photographs, illustrations or other non-textual material prepared for your book cover. Artwork can relate to the ebook cover and the whole paperback cover.

**Bleed:** The area of your print that will be cut off during the trimming process. It is essentially an extension of your artwork beyond your chosen trim size, and is usually 0.125 inches on every side (height and width).

**Brief:** A brief is a set of instructions for your designer and contains general information about your book, such as the title and synopsis, as well as details on characters, scenes and genre.

**CMYK:** This is a colour profile required for printed materials. It is an abbreviation of cyan, magenta, yellow and key (black).

**Colour wheel:** A circle with different coloured sections to show the relationships between colours.

**Commission:** To commission, or commissioning, a piece of artwork is the act of hiring a designer for the purpose of designing your book cover.

**Copyright:** Unless specified in a contract to the contrary, copyright is the exclusive legal right given to the client of a commissioned artwork or artistic material. For more details, read the chapter titled *Copyright*.

**Crop:** to cut a piece of artwork, such as your ebook cover, to its trim size.

**Design software:** Image-editing software used to alter and create digital imagery. Examples include Photoshop and GIMP.

**DPI:** This is an abbreviation of dots per inch, and regards the amount of pixels used in an inch. Printed materials require a minimum of 300 dpi, whereas web-based images only need 72 dpi.

**Familiarity theory:** The theory that emulating a design aesthetic within a genre, especially an aesthetic that is

successful, is more beneficial than standing out from
your genre.

**Flatten:** To compress your Photoshop file and its layers into
one document.

**Font:** Strictly speaking, a specific style of typeface. Such as
bold, oblique or condensed.

**Free-form drawing:** Using the cursor on your screen to draw
directly onto your artwork, often using a pen or brush tool
within your design software.

**Google Fonts:** A collection of royalty-free fonts by Google
initially created for web and available to download from
fonts.google.com.

**High-resolution images:** Often abbreviated to 'hi-res', these
images use 300 dpi or more and are perfect for both printed
and digital artwork.

**InDesign:** A desktop publishing software application created
by Adobe. It can be used to create works such as posters,
brochures and book covers.

**Jpeg:** A format for compressing an image and often used for
digital files such as your ebook.

**Keyword:** A word or phrase used while searching for an
image on a stock image site.

**Layer mask:** An addition to a layer that allows you to remove and replace areas of artwork without permanently affecting the layer itself.

**Layer:** In design software, a layer is the term used to describe the separate objects, text and images which are used in your artwork. They can be moved in hierarchy and can be switched on or off.

**Layered file:** A term used for artwork using a series of layers.

**Low-resolution images:** Often abbreviated to low-res, these images are below 300 dpi and are usually set at 72 dpi. Images that are low-res are perfect for your ebook and website.

**PDF:** A PDF (portable document format) is a file format for sending electronic documents in an exact specification.

**Photoshop:** Adobe's image-editing software for digitally altering and designing artwork.

**Picture research:** The process of finding the right images or illustrations for your book cover.

**Pixel:** A single and tiny area of illumination on a screen and the basic unit of programmable colour on a screen or display.

**Pixelate:** When enlarging a low-resolution image the individual pixels, which appear square in shape, become apparent and the detail of the original image becomes 'blocky' in appearance.

**PPI:** This stands for pixels per inch and is another term for dpi.

**Raster images:** Also called bitmap graphics, these are digital images composed of pixels, which form an image.

**Retouching:** Using your design software to make additions and corrections to an image or illustration, such as defining a figure or removing a feature of an image.

**RGB:** The colour profile using red, green, and blue. Predominantly used for digital-based files such as your ebook.

**Rights-managed:** A copyright license on an image or illustration for one-time use over a specified period.

**Royalty-free:** Copyright on an image or illustration without the constraints of license fees or paying royalties.

**Self-Publishing Formula:** A company created by Mark Dawson that produce a series of courses, podcasts and information for independent authors.

**Spine width:** The width calculated using the thickness of paper, trim size and page count.

**Stock image site / Image library:** A searchable website of photography and illustrations where an image can be purchased or licensed for a various uses.

**Trim size:** The intended and final height and width of your book after it has been bound and trimmed.

**Typeface:** The term for a particular design of type, such as Helvetica or Garamond.

**Vector images:** An image format not defined by pixels, which instead uses a series of paths to create any number of shapes. The benefit of vector images is that they can be enlarged without any loss of quality.

**Watermark:** A logo or word (often the brand of a stock library) written across a sample image to protect the image from being stolen or used without permission.

# SUBSCRIBE

**Be the first to hear about discounts, new pre-made designs and more! Subscribe now and never miss an update.**

Building a relationship with my readers and clients is one of the best things about working in self-publishing and cover design. I occasionally send newsletters with special offers for my book cover design course, brand new pre-made covers I have added to my store, and other bits of news relating to cover design.

If you would like to sign-up, simply use this link: www.bookscovered.co.uk/subscribe

P.S. You can unsubscribe at any time.

## ABOUT THE AUTHOR

Stuart Bache is the Art Director and founder of Books Covered, the book cover design agency for self-published authors. He has worked across almost every genre for all the major publishers and for many authors. He lives in Shrewsbury with his wife and daughter.

You can work with Stuart and his company by sending an email here: www.bookscovered.co.uk/contact

 facebook.com/bookscovered

twitter.com/StuartBache

Made in the USA
Middletown, DE
03 February 2019